Original title:
Citrus Delight

Copyright © 2025 Creative Arts Management OÜ
All rights reserved.

Author: Nora Sinclair
ISBN HARDBACK: 978-1-80586-255-0
ISBN PAPERBACK: 978-1-80586-727-2

Blush of the Tangerine Twilight

In the glow of twilight's cheer,
Tangerines roll, now come near.
They giggle in the orange hue,
Tickling toes, just for you.

They dance in bowls, a zesty show,
With peels that laugh, and juice that flows.
Each slice is wild, a burst of fun,
Who knew a fruit could be this pun?

Fragments of Sweet Sunshine.

Lemon drops rain from the sky,
With a twist of fate, oh me, oh my!
Limes make faces, sour and bright,
While berries blush in sheer delight.

Oranges wear their zest with pride,
Chasing shadows, they cannot hide.
With every bite, a chuckle's found,
In juicy realms, we're all spellbound!

Sunshine in a Zest

A funky fruit with zest so bold,
Grapefruits giggle, tales untold.
A splash of sweet, a bite of zest,
Why wear a frown when you can jest?

Under the sun, they leap and bounce,
Lemonheads wear a goofy pounce.
In every sip, a wink and grin,
A juicy riot, let the fun begin!

Tangy Whispers of Spring

Spring arrives with bright confetti,
Mandarins drop, all loose and ready.
Whispers of tang in the air,
Even the squirrels start to share.

A playful burst, a sweet parade,
Lively fruits in frolic displayed.
With every slice, laughter swells,
In our citrus world, fun dwells!

Citrus Tango

Oranges in hats, lemons in shoes,
Dancing around, spilling their juice.
Limes roll by, trying to keep pace,
With grapefruits twirling, they join the race.

Tangerines giggle, swinging so low,
They trip on their peels, oh, don't steal the show!
All in a whirl, what a juicy sight,
In the wacky groove of a fruity night.

Sweetness in a Peel

Why did the lemon always wear a grin?
It knew that sweetness was hiding within!
Peeling away worries, unwrapping the fun,
With each slice of life, brighter than the sun.

The orange sang loudly, a bold serenade,
While the lime played the tambourine, unafraid.
They formed a band, those zany zesters,
Creating a tune that no one could test for!

Orchard Rhythms

In a garden so wild, the fruits have a beat,
The apples get jiggy, they can't take a seat.
With pears in the mix, doing the split,
Nothing goes wrong when you're fruity and lit.

Join the dance party, grab a whole crew,
The figs bring the rhythm, the cherries bring hue.
With every sweet note, and every sip served,
Life's just a dance with every curve served!

The Joy of Zest

Zesty and bright, it's a citrus parade,
With lemon confetti, who could be afraid?
Limes squeeze a joke, the laughter will burst,
In this zany world, you'll find all the firsts.

A splash of surprise in every bright bite,
The grapefruit winks, all gleeful and bright.
A toast with the peels, let the fun never cease,
In this zesty delight, there's always more peace!

Golden Drops of Joy

In the garden, lemons giggle,
Their zest a mischievous wiggle.
Oranges plot with sly delight,
While grapefruits dance, oh what a sight!

Limes wear hats, so very bright,
They toast to laughter, day and night.
A tangerine trips, falls on its peel,
Rolling around, what a fruity deal!

Citrus Symphony

A symphony of colors play,
With every wedge, we laugh and sway.
A key lime pie, a sweetened jest,
Lemonade quips with every zest!

The oranges hum, a catchy tune,
While juicy notes burst, like balloons.
Grapefruit's jokes are a bit too tart,
Yet they charm every giggling heart!

The Orchard's Palette

In the orchard, colors bloom,
With fruity friends, there's always room.
Yellow cheer and orange wit,
Bouncing laughter, never quit!

Limes are the jesters, of course,
Squeezing jokes with little force.
Mandarins giggle, sharing glee,
While peels slip underfoot in spree!

Squeezed Sunshine

Sunshine's squeezed in every drop,
Making laughter rise and hop.
A glass of joy on a summer day,
With silly puns that come out to play!

Pineapple joins, it's quite the mix,
With jokes about coconut tricks.
Zesty vibes in the midday sun,
In this fruity world, we have such fun!

Zesty Whispers of Sunshine

Lemons giggle on the trees,
They dance around with buzzing bees.
Oranges roll, a playful race,
Lime's a joker, full of grace.

Citrus hats upon the ground,
Twirling in a merry round.
Each fruit strides with wobbly cheer,
Laughing at the world, my dear.

Orchard's Sweet Lament

A grapefruit sings a sad, soft tune,
Wishing for a sunny afternoon.
Tangerines wear frowns so round,
While kumquats roam the orchard ground.

Their peels are rough, but hearts are light,
Fruity sorrows take to flight.
Pineapples dance with a silly sway,
Dreaming of a better day.

Tangy Dreams in Golden Hues

Mangoes prance with a sultry grin,
While limes compete for the fresh win.
Papayas roll in colorful bunch,
Declaring laughter over lunch.

Citron's charm will steal the show,
With zestiness that's sure to grow.
Sweetness basking in the sun,
In this orchard, life's all fun.

Squeeze of Summer's Embrace

A juicy splash, a zesty cheer,
Sticky fingers, nothing to fear.
Fruits collide in a playful fight,
Citrus chaos, pure delight.

The tangy taste of summer's kiss,
Brings giggles that I can't dismiss.
From sunup to the stars above,
These silly fruits spread all the love.

Glistening Juices

In the fridge, a beast resides,
With zesty shades that play and glide.
I reach for it, my heart a rave,
But slip and slip—oh, what a wave!

A splash of orange on my shoe,
The fruit once proud, now just a goo.
I laugh and dance, my troubles gone,
In the kitchen, I'm a fruit-fueled fawn!

The blender roars, a merry tune,
While lemons plot their bright monsoon.
I squeeze and swirl, a funny show,
And watch my snack begin to glow!

With each slice, the laughter grows,
Invisible gnomes sneak in my prose.
I take a sip; it's love at last,
And toast to joy in every blast!

The Echo of Citrus

A jolly orange rolls away,
I chase it down—a merry play!
It bounces high, it spins around,
While I'm just stuck here on the ground!

Lemons giggle from their bowl,
Grapefruit claims to have a soul.
"Join the party!" they all yell,
As if I could—oh, what the hell!

The zestful dance upon my face,
Each sip a splash, a fruity chase.
I slip and slide, I laugh so free,
Behold the joy of jubilee!

And when I try to take a bite,
The pulp explodes—what pure delight!
My friends all gasp, then burst with cheer,
Mocking me with every sneer!

Sweet Tang of Awakening

Morning sun with citrus frowns,
I sip my juice—now wearing crowns!
Pineapple tropes and orange streaks,
In my dreams, they dance and squeak!

A sprightly lime joins in the fun,
"Let's play tag!" it shouts, then runs.
I dodge and dive, my slippers squeal,
As I chase that juicy wheel!

The bouncing berries sing a song,
While I just bumble, getting wronged.
I try to juggle fruits galore,
But down they plummet; what a roar!

Yet still I laugh amidst the mess,
The zesty chaos brings me blessed.
With every sip, my laughter swells,
In my fresh world, all is well!

Tangelo Tango

A tangelo twisted, what a sight,
It danced on the table, oh what a plight.
With zesty moves, it took a chance,
Spinning and rolling in a citrus dance.

Neighbors peeked in, with a raise of an eye,
Wondering how that fruit learned to fly.
It twirled and it swayed, a juicy charmer,
Who knew fruit could be such a farmer?

Lemonade Days

Oh, the days when the sun turns bright,
Lemonade stands pop up, what a delight.
Sipping on sweetness, a splash on my nose,
With giggles and snorts, anything goes.

The lemons conspired, they laughed in the jug,
Wiggling and jiggling, giving a shrug.
A tart little twist, a giggle galore,
A sip from the cup, and I'm ready for more!

A Splash of Citrus

With a splash of zest, the party begins,
Orange juice rivers, swimming with sins.
Toss in a grapefruit, watch them collide,
Bouncing around like a wild carnival ride.

Limes in the corner, with hats askew,
They giggle and laugh, 'What shall we do?'
A splash here, a squirt there, a fruity parade,
It's all just a hullabaloo, none dismayed!

Orange Blossom Breeze

In the calm of the breeze, the oranges sing,
Swinging from branches, what joy do they bring!
One took a tumble, rolled right on by,
Chasing the wind, a silly goodbye.

The blossoms were laughing, blossoms were cheerin',
While bees buzzed around, "What's all this here 'in?"
A fruity fiasco, a burst of delight,
Who knew 'round fruit trees, fun could take flight?

Whirlwind of Flavors

In a jar of jam, a dance occurs,
Lemons twist, and oranges purr.
Grapefruits giggle, limes take a spin,
Fruit salad party, let the fun begin!

With a splash, a zest so bright,
Twirling taste buds, pure delight.
Sippin' joy in every bite,
Fruit frolics through the moonlit night!

Orchard Reverie

In the orchard's sway, we climb so high,
Picking oranges as the birds fly by.
Witty lemons shout, 'Hey, don't forget!',
'The juiciness beckons, come join our set!'

Peeling joy, the laughter spills,
As grapefruits bounce like little hills.
Covered in juice, a sticky affair,
Squeezed by giggles, we dance without care!

Golden Drops of Happiness

A sunny sip of lemonade,
Pours laughter on a summer parade.
Marmalade wiggles, spreads the cheer,
While zesty whispers tickle the ear!

Tangerines throw confetti in the air,
As we juggle fruits without a care.
Oh, the sweetness, it drips and flows,
Beneath the sun, our humor grows!

Taste of a Tangy Love

She said, 'I love you like a lime,
Sour and sweet, it's the perfect rhyme.'
Together we squeezed, oh what a sight,
Sipping our love beneath the twilight!

With every slice, our hearts collide,
In a zestful hug, we take a ride.
Peel back the layers, reveal the fun,
In a tangy embrace, we become one!

Sweetened Sunshine

In a world of zest and cheer,
Lemons and limes, they appear.
Dancing on forks, they laugh and play,
Wobbling jellies in a bright display.

Oranges slip with giggles galore,
Tangerines roll right out the door.
Lemonade rivers flowing so sweet,
With sugar-a-plenty, it can't be beat!

Meringue clouds drift in the air,
Citron dreams beyond compare.
Lime pies wink with cheeky grins,
While grapefruits plot their playful spins.

Sips of Citrus Bliss

With a crunch of zest in each bold sip,
Tropical fruits take us on a trip.
Fizzy joy in every pour,
Mimosa dances, who could ask for more?

A citrus party in every glass,
Where even the limes like to amass.
Fanny packs and sun hats get along,
As oranges sing their zesty song.

Side by side, they mingle and meet,
In papaya's charm, they twirl and greet.
Tiny umbrellas caught in a whirl,
As waves of flavor around us swirl.

Blossoms in the Sun

Blooms of color, a vibrant spree,
Zesty flowers buzzing with glee.
Buzzing bees do the cha-cha dance,
While fruit in sunbeams takes a chance.

Lemon-scented breezes collide,
With joyful colors they take pride.
Fruits parade with sparkly flair,
Showing off their zestful hair.

Sunshine giggles, tickled by fruit,
As peaches swing in their floral suit.
Orange petals wave from above,
Inviting us into their world of love.

Juicy Whimsy

Bouncing lemons in a playful race,
Slipping on peels, oh what a place!
Limes are giggling, as they do zoom,
Creating chaos in the kitchen room.

With a burst of color, fruits hold sway,
In this zesty kingdom, they laugh and play.
Meringue clouds float, no cares to weigh,
Jelly jiggling in the fruity ballet.

Pineapples prance, tops held high,
While cherries blush and wave goodbye.
Bananas join with a slippery cheer,
As a wild fruit dance draws everyone near.

The Dance of Ripe Orbs

In orchards bright with golden hue,
The rinds do jig, a lively crew.
They wobble, bounce, or flap a wing,
A fruit parade, oh what a thing!

With laughter loud, they twist and sway,
A tango zestful, come what may.
The grapefruits giggle, lemons tease,
While limes just roll with perfect ease.

A slice of fun, with juice around,
They tumble forth and hit the ground.
A fruitful mess, but no distress,
For who could frown at such a jest?

So join the dance, let worries cease,
With every hop, find citrus peace.
Life's a ball when fruits conspire,
To set our hearts and laughter higher!

The Scent of Joyful Harvest

The fields are ripe with scents divine,
Where zestful fragrances entwine.
A bounty bright, with twist and cheer,
Eager noses draw you near.

A splash of zest and laughter swells,
Perfumed joy in orchard shells.
With tiny insects buzzing close,
They sip on nectar, like a ghost.

But watch your step, the squishy ground,
A playful slip, and off you bound!
Rolling 'neath the sunlit sky,
With every giggle, let out a sigh.

So raise a glass of tangy glee,
In every sip, pure jubilee.
A cheerful toast, let laughter start,
As fruits unite and warm the heart!

Bitter Sweetness Under the Sun

Beneath the sun, a twist of fate,
A tarty lemon's on a plate.
With humor sharp, it cuts the air,
Like lookin' at a sour bear.

The oranges grin, a peppy bunch,
While limes are poised to pack a punch.
Each juicy jest, a zesty tease,
A jester's game, with wit to please.

But watch your face with each first bite,
A puckered look, such silly sight!
Sweet moments blend with tangy fun,
Life's a circus under the sun.

Yet through the clash, find laughter's key,
In bitter fruits, pure ecstasy.
So dance along, with zestful flair,
For sweetness lurks everywhere!

Floral Notes in a Fruitful Harmony

Amidst the blooms, the fruits convene,
With floral notes, a vibrant scene.
The oranges hum a sunny tune,
While blossoms sway and dance in June.

A zesty breeze begins to play,
As honey bees join in the fray.
They buzz along, like little jesters,
In gardens bright, they're true investors.

A splash of color, a playful jest,
Green leaves clap, they're feeling blessed.
Where nectar flows and laughter spins,
In every bloom, the glee begins.

So pluck a fruit, take joy above,
In every bite, find laughter's love.
A fruitful symphony of cheer,
With floral notes, let's persevere!

A Citrus Carnival

Oranges juggle on a clown's nose,
Lemons twirl in a dizzy pose,
Limes leap high in joyful play,
Grapefruits bounce, hip-hip-hooray!

Sour faces turn to glee,
Juicy laughs from every tree,
Tangerine pies spin and fly,
In this circus, fruit can't lie!

A parade of zest, what a sight,
Limes all dressed in shades so bright,
With zestful beats and fruity rhymes,
They rhythmically dance, losing time!

Come one, come all, no need to pout,
In this carnival, there's no doubt,
With whimsy fruit and laughter loud,
We'll make our sour friends so proud!

Sunlit Fragments

In the sun, a zestful dream,
Lemonade flows like a stream,
Limes wear shades, oh what a sight,
Dancing shadows, pure delight!

Orange balloons float past my head,
Silly thoughts, they fill my bread,
Every sip, a giggle's burst,
With every twist, I quench my thirst!

Tartness tickles on my tongue,
While limes and lemons sing their song,
Mimosa frogs jump with delight,
Making breakfast feel just right!

With each fragment, laughter grows,
In these moments, joy just flows,
Sunlit fragments, bright and new,
Sour surprise, a happy brew!

Sweet and Sour Sunshine

Sunshine giggles, bright and loud,
Sour faces in the crowd,
Sweet and tart, a funny clash,
As watermelons fall with a splash!

Pineapples dance in bowler hats,
While grapefruits spin like acrobats,
With fruity pies, they take a dive,
In this banquet—who will survive?

Lemon zests do wacky flips,
Bananas join with silly quips,
A mishmash of fruity fun,
Our laughter shines like golden sun!

Sweet and sour, life's best game,
In this wacky fruit-filled frame,
With every twist, a giggle grows,
Sunshine bursts, and laughter glows!

Citrus Serenade

A merry tune of fruit we play,
Lemons laugh and cheer hooray,
Limes in chorus call and sing,
As grapefruit croons of zesty spring!

Orange notes jump to the beat,
Dancing toes and wiggly feet,
Pies parade down sunny lanes,
Every bite, a burst of gains!

With every strum of tangy zest,
We shake our hips and feel so blessed,
Sour giggles whirl 'round in glee,
A serenade of fruity spree!

Slice and dice, the music's right,
In this comedy of light,
With a citrus flair, we serenade,
In this funny, fruity escapade!

Grove of Vibrant Treasures

In a grove so bright, the fruit does glow,
Lemons laugh and oranges stow.
Tangerines dance in the evening breeze,
Mischievous limes hide behind the trees.

Bobbing fruits with giggles galore,
Juggling jokes and pranks to explore.
Chasing each other in playful delight,
Under the sun, everything feels right.

Swinging high, the branches sway,
The fruits are lively, brightening the day.
With every squeeze, a chuckle is heard,
In this grove, joy is always preferred.

Twilight of the Citrus Grove

As twilight falls, the colors blend,
Fruits in the orchard plot a silly trend.
Orange moon smiles, a wink of zest,
Lemons roll, playing jest after jest.

Limes laugh loudly, a snooze in the hay,
Tangerines tossing, come join the play!
While grapefruits giggle from branches so high,
The stars start to twinkle, almost shy.

The fruits all gather, sharing a tale,
Of sticky fingers and sweet lemonade fail.
Under the stars, their antics unfold,
In a twilight dance, a story retold.

Lemonade Journals

Notebooks filled with funny tales,
Of juicy tricks and fruity fails.
Pages stained with sticky delight,
Laughs spill like juice, oh what a sight!

A squirt from a lemon, a fizzling cough,
Grapefruit giggles would never scoff.
Each splash tells a story, quirky and bright,
In this zesty journal, laughter takes flight.

Scribbles of joy in every bite,
Mixing memories, both sour and right.
Pickled puns and pineapple praise,
In a world so fruity, we happily gaze.

A Plethora of Peels

Peels on the floor, a slippery scene,
Fruits in a frenzy, just like a dream.
Bananas slip, oh what a show,
Tangerines tumble, round they go!

Spinning like tops, the fruits take a dive,
A fruit salad circus, keeping alive.
Grapes roll by in a purple parade,
While oranges plot, a juicy brigade.

On this wild ride, the laughter is bold,
Sharing sweet tales never grow old.
With every peel, a giggle escapes,
In the wild orchard, pure joy shapes.

Sweet Slices of Sun

Lemon drops shining like little suns,
Limes with their giggles, oh what fun!
Oranges roll in a playful race,
Chasing each other, a fruity embrace.

Grapefruit grins, so bitter-sweet,
Telling bad jokes, trying to compete.
Tangerines dance with a zestful flair,
In the fruit bowl, they're the life, I swear!

Bright Ambrosia

Slices of orange, a juicy tease,
Trying to convince me to take a squeeze.
Pineapple winks with a golden hue,
Saying, "Hey buddy, I'm good for you!"

Mangoes splash in tropical glee,
Looking for friends, come climb a tree.
Beneath the sun with laughter so loud,
These sweet treats surely make me proud!

Zesty Serenade

A tangerine sings with a cheeky song,
About how fruit can never go wrong.
Lemonade dreams drip on the floor,
Who knew these fruits could be so hardcore?

Limes like to rhyme and always have fun,
Joking that life is a giant pun.
Passionfruit whispers, "Join in my spree!"
As we laugh under the fruity marquee!

Peel Back the Layers

A grapefruit's hat is a twisty peel,
He tells me secrets, trying to feel.
Oranges chuckle, their smiles so bright,
"Life is just sweetness, what a delight!"

Bananas slip with a wink and a jig,
"Who needs a stage, I'll dance a big gig!"
Citrus peels laughter, a funny charade,
In the orchard, where joy is displayed!

Sun-Kissed Juices

A splash of yellow on my face,
The sun thinks it's a race.
With every squeeze, a giggle flows,
As juicy sunshine overflows.

My friend, the orange, wears a grin,
Laughing as I squeeze him in.
Lemon's sour, but jokes are sweet,
In this fruit bowl, we can't be beat!

A fruity dance, a zesty whirl,
Sipping joy, away we twirl.
When life gives fruit, I prance around,
In this garden, laughter's found.

So let's raise a glass, it's time to cheer,
With every drop, we spread the cheer.
A toast to juices, bright and bold,
In laughter's grip, we never grow old!

Fragrant Pages of Lemon Gold

Turn the page, a world of zest,
With every slice, we feel the best.
Lemon chapters filled with cheer,
A story served with lemonade near.

Each word is tangy, sharp yet sweet,
As laughter dances on our feet.
Orange lines twist, and lime confides,
In this fruity tale, joy resides.

With every chapter, a citrus thrill,
Page by page, we drink our fill.
It's a book where jokes abound,
In the margins, giggles are found.

So grab a slice, sit down, unwind,
In this fruity realm, peace you'll find.
A page-turner of sunshine fun,
Each slice a story, laughter's run!

A Symphony of Sweet and Sour

In orchards where the flavors blend,
A symphony where fruits transcend.
Sweet notes dance with a sour twist,
In every drop, I can't resist.

Lemon trumpets play a tune,
Orange violins make flowers bloom.
Together they create a show,
A juicy concert, let it flow!

Pineapple joins with a tropical beat,
While lime laughs, a tangy treat.
Citrus melodies fill the air,
As we twirl like we haven't a care.

So let the fruits lead the way,
On this zesty, fruity play.
With every sip, the laughter pours,
In this symphony, joy restores!

Limoncello Serenade

Under moonlight, it starts to shine,
A golden drink that's oh-so-fine.
With every sip, a wink and smile,
This limoncello makes life worthwhile.

Chilled and sweet, it takes the stage,
With zesty laughter, we engage.
A serenade in a crystal glass,
With every gulp, the moments pass.

Friends gather 'round, a festive cheer,
"More, please!" we shout, we persevere.
A night of fun, with fruit so bright,
As laughter dances in the moonlight.

Raise your glass to joyfulness,
To zesty nights, to laughter's caress.
This sweet serenade won't fade away,
In our hearts, it'll always stay!

Sun-Drenched Delights

Beneath the sun's bright glare, they play,
A lemon wearing shades, so gay!
A lime did cartwheels on a floor,
While oranges called for one encore.

Grapefruits in hats, oh what a sight,
Running races, what a delight!
They toss their peels like confetti flies,
Amidst the laughter, their joy multiplies.

Lemonade showers from the sky,
The fruit parade goes rolling by!
With giggles and grins, they spin around,
In fruitopia, happiness is found.

So raise a glass, let's have our cheer,
To fruity fun, let's persevere!
In this zesty land, we twirl and glide,
Life's tart and sweet, just like a ride!

The Tale of the Tangerine

Once there was a tangerine so round,
With a laugh that echoed all around.
He dreamt of being a big dessert,
But slipped on peel, oh what a hurt!

He rolled to a party with fateful glee,
Mistook the punch for a bowl of tea.
He splashed and danced, oh what a scene,
Turned into a fruity, jolly machine!

With each misstep, the crowd would roar,
"Be careful, buddy, don't hit the floor!"
But our tangerine shrugged, "I'll take a chance,
Life's a dance, let's wobble and prance!"

So if ever you see the fruit, so bright,
Join in the fun, be merry tonight!
With tangerines all wrapped with glee,
Who knew being fruit could be so free?

Zestful Dreams

In a land of zest, where fruits do sing,
A grapefruit wore a crown, 'how quaint' the bling!
The limes in the corner played a game,
Of hide and seek, but who's to blame?

The oranges danced, twirling in the breeze,
Sporting fluffy socks and mismatched knees.
A peach came along, waving with flair,
"Come join the fun, if you dare!"

Then a whisper arose from a curious lime,
"What if we juggle? We've got time!"
With peels a-toss, the laughter erupted,
As citrus dreams left all interrupted.

So let's take a trip down fruity lane,
Where every giggle is a sweet refrain.
With zest in our hearts, we'll laugh and gleam,
In this wacky world of zesty dreams!

Citrus Chronicles

Gather 'round, my juicy friends,
For tales of zest that never ends.
With lemons plotting their grand escape,
And limes disguising in great shape.

One day they hatched a brilliant scheme,
To roll downtown, it was supreme!
They rounded a corner, oh what a scene,
An orange slipped in his new machine!

With every bump, they laughed so loud,
They stirred a fruit-party, drew a crowd.
The grape embossed the outer shell,
And sang a tune, oh, so swell!

So remember, dear, the fun we hold,
When zesty fruit lets loose and bold.
From laughter shared to adventures grand,
These fruity chronicles forever stand!

Bright and Bold

A lemon wore a silly hat,
Said, "I'm the king, what's wrong with that?"
An orange danced with glee and flair,
"I'm the star, but I don't care!"

A lime rolled by, all dressed in green,
Claimed the crown was meant for a queen.
Ripe and juicy, they chuckled loud,
In their fruity kingdom, oh so proud!

Grapefruit chimed in with a hearty laugh,
Said, "I'm the punchline, do the math!"
Together they formed a fruity crew,
Each with quirks, and spritz of dew!

So come and join this jolly parade,
With zest and humor, never fade!
In this orchard of laughter and cheer,
Fruits unite, the fun is here!

Citrus Colors Unwrapped

An orange showed up with a wig on tight,
Claiming it shimmered in the moonlight.
A lemon laughed, 'You look quite absurd,
But that's the funniest thing I've heard!'

A tangerine twirled, feeling quite posh,
Bouncing around, an aromatic swash!
With every jig, a pitiful slip,
But laughter erupted at each funny flip!

"I'm zestier than you!" the lime took a stand,
Mashed itself into a fruit band!
Squished together, they sang a tune,
Underneath the bright, laughing moon!

Their colors bright, each peel so bold,
Every tale a delight to be told.
In this jolly patch of fruit-filled fun,
The party's just started, not yet done!

Whispers of the Orchard

In the orchard, a banana made a call,
'Who's the silliest of us all?'
A kiwi chimed in, unpeeling with glee,
'I think it's me, come see, come see!'

A bunch of grapes giggled, dangling near,
'We've got the juice, let's cheer and cheer!'
One grape stumbled, fell to the ground,
'Hey, don't squish me!' was the funny sound!

Oranges stacked high on a fruit-filled shelf,
Huddled and whispered, 'Let's be ourselves!'
'At this fruity forum, no need for pose,
With laughter and fun, that's how it goes!'

So in this orchard where laughter grows,
The fruits don bright, funny clothes.
With each joyous whisper and giggling shout,
They spread cheer, that's what it's about!

Radiant Fruit Harmony

Maraschino cherries threw a dance,
In bright red skirts, they took a chance!
A pear tried to join but tripped on its stem,
The fruits all giggled at the silly gem!

A watermelon rolled and made a grand splash,
Said, 'I'm the coolest, in a juicy flash!'
But the others just quacked like ducks in a row,
Laughter erupted, in a fruit-filled show!

'We're the funniest bunch on the block!'
An apple declared, with a playful shock!
'With vibrant colors and zest that's bold,
This harmony of laughter never gets old!'

So let's lift our glasses and toast with cheer,
To funny fruits, bringing joy near!
In this radiant rhythm, we dance and sway,
With laughter, we brighten each sunny day!

A Juicy Journey

In a world of tart and sweet,
I tripped on a wedge, oh what a feat!
With oranges rolling, I danced in glee,
My laughter echoed, oh can't you see?

Lemonade rivers flowed down the street,
I slipped on a slice, that's hard to beat!
Grapefruit giggles bounced in the air,
As I tumbled, no worries, no care.

Tangerine dreams filled my head,
With every bounce, more juice was shed!
I painted the town in shades of zest,
With my juicy journey, I felt blessed.

Now I wear peels like a crown,
Juicy fun, I'd never frown!
In this fruity land, I reign supreme,
With every giggle, I live the dream.

Slices of Sunshine

Under the bright, merry sun,
I found a slice, oh what fun!
Lemons laughing, oranges cheer,
With a zesty grin, I draw near.

In a bowl of fruit, I take a dive,
The sweetest giggles come alive!
Juicy laughter in every bite,
With each slice, I feel so light.

With my friends, we peel and share,
As citrus puns fill the air!
We juggle limes 'til we all fall,
In this sunny slice, we have a ball!

With zest in our hearts, we play all day,
In fruity fun, who needs delay?
We dance and twirl 'round in the sun,
In Slices of Sunshine, we're never done.

The Zestful Heart

My heart is fresh like a lemon's glow,
With every beat, I dance and flow!
A twist of lime, a splash of cheer,
With every zesty hug, I draw near.

Oranges in my pocket, what a find,
I squeeze one, and joy entwined!
With every chuckle, a seed takes flight,
My zestful heart bursts day and night.

I wear a smile like a juicy peel,
In this world, it's such a deal!
With laughter bright, I skip about,
In playful shouts, I twist and shout!

So join my fun, let the laughter start,
Together, we've got a zestful heart!
With every citrus flirt, we'll prance,
In this game of joy, let's take a chance!

Orchard's Glow

In an orchard bright, full of cheer,
I climbed a tree with no fear!
The branches swayed, a fruity dance,
In this zesty world, I took my chance.

Lemons winked from a sunlit bough,
While oranges nudged, 'Come on, wow!'
With every giggle, a juicy splash,
In Orchard's Glow, we made a crash!

I slipped and slid on a grapefruit slide,
With rinds of laughter, I took the ride.
In this fruity realm, so free and bold,
With every twist, a story told.

So if you find a spot that glows,
Join me where the laughter flows!
In juicy fun, let's gather round,
In Orchard's Glow, our joy is found.

An Orchard's Glow

In the garden, fruit does dance,
Lemon peels in a lively prance,
Oranges giggle in the tree,
While limes play hide and seek with glee.

Tangerines roll down the hill,
Chasing birds; they run and spill,
Grapefruits wear a goofy grin,
As they bounce and cheer, let the fun begin.

A fruit parade, so sweet, so bright,
Each round fellow chasing the light,
With every squeeze, a burst of cheer,
Stirring laughter, far and near.

Underneath the sun's warm rays,
These jolly jewels sparkle and play,
Let's gather round, don't be shy,
In this orchard, joy will fly!

The Cheery Citron

There's a citron, round and bold,
With a smile worth more than gold,
Dancing in the summer breeze,
Waving at the humming bees.

A chatty fruit, she tells a tale,
Of lemon pranks and orange mail,
With each witty word, she lights the day,
Making sour things fade away.

Juicy jokes in every slice,
Sour laughs, oh, they're so nice,
Her zestful charm can lift the gloom,
Turning frowns into a bloom!

With her friends, the fruits unite,
Kicking back in pure delight,
Join the fun, let laughter unfold,
With the cheery citron, brave and bold!

Fresh Squeeze Serenade

A squeeze of zest, a splash of cheer,
With quirky fruit friends gathered near,
Limes strum tunes on tiny strings,
While oranges dance, flapping their wings.

Each slice a note, sweet symphony,
Lemon duets with harmony,
Mangoes sway to the rhythm's beat,
As grapefruits twirl on their happy feet.

Pineapples hum a tropical song,
Bananas join in, all sing along,
With laughter bursting like fresh juice,
This fruity fun, we can't excuse!

So bring your cups, we're on a spree,
In this concert full of glee,
Every drop, a memory made,
In this fresh squeeze serenade.

Sunlit Gems

In a sunlit grove, bright fruits collide,
Playing tag, what a joyful ride,
Pineapples chuckle, apples cheer,
While cherries giggle, bringing the near.

A playful lemon loses its hat,
Rolling by, "Oh, no!" – how about that?
Kiwis bounce, showing off their fuzz,
While playful plums create a buzz!

Then a grapefruit, looking quite sly,
Tricks a peach, oh me, oh my!
"Can't catch me!" the fruits declare,
As sunlit gems dance through the air.

So take your time, join the parade,
In this orchard where joy is made,
With vibrant colors and laughter learned,
Sunlit gems, our hearts they've turned!

Sun-soaked Citrus Kisses

A lemon danced with a cheeky grin,
Wiggling its peel, let the fun begin.
An orange rolled in with a splashy cheer,
"I'm zesty and bright, just want some beer!"

A grapefruit laughed, full of tart delight,
"I'll mix with your juice, make the party bright!"
They tossed all their seeds with a giggling shout,
Little pips flew away, scattering about!

Limes squeezed in jokes, they were quite absurd,
"I'm the punchline here, haven't you heard?"
With zest they all joked, a fruity parade,
A carnival of flavors, no one was afraid!

So here's to the fruits, in their silly spree,
Their laughter echoed, wild and free.
Under the sun, they danced all day,
In a world made of zest, come play, come play!

Aroma of a Juicy Morning

A whiff from the kitchen, oh what a scene,
Pineapple sassy, wearing a sheen.
"Breakfast is calling, come rise and shine!"
Said kiwi so slyly, "A toast with fine wine!"

Mornings were wild, with fruit in a bowl,
Bananas did merry dances, on a roll.
"I'm the star here!" they bellowed with glee,
"In this fruity fiesta, come feast with me!"

Papaya took charge, with a whirl and a spin,
"Who wants a smoothie? Let the fun begin!"
They blended and frothed, splashing with style,
Fruit mischief brewed, bringing laughter worthwhile!

So raise up your glasses, let's toast to the morn,
When fruit rules the kitchen, new fun is born.
Let's savor the joy, with each juicy bite,
In the aroma of mornings, everything's bright!

Pith and Promise

An orange was grinning with zest in its eyes,
"I'm here for the laughs, and the sticky goodbyes!"
A lime piped up, with its cheeky cheek,
"Let's roll and get funky, it's fun that we seek!"

With pithy remarks, they bantered and played,
Witty little jokes, that never did fade.
"We'll squeeze out the giggles, have juice on the side,
In this fruity circus, let's all take a ride!"

Tangerines twirled, a sweet little crew,
"We bring the sunshine, the golden hue!"
Together they hatched quite the juicy scheme,
Filling the air with a fruity dream!

So raise up your peels, come join in the fun,
With pith and promise, the laughter has spun.
In this zesty gathering, let's feast on the cheer,
For every fruit's silly, they have no fear!

Dappled Light Through the Leaves

A tangy lemon spotted, basking in rays,
"I brighten your day in so many ways!"
Under dappled light, a grapefruit sang,
"With my pom-pom-shaped self, hear the joy I clang!"

A lime made a face, all puckered and sweet,
"Let's serve up some laughter, a fruity treat!"
Bouncing on branches, like kids in a park,
They giggled and jostled, from dawn until dark!

Through leaves filled with laughter, the sunlight did play,

With sweet little banter, to brighten the day.
Together they twirled, a merry parade,
In a dappled delight, their whims were displayed!

So here's to the orchard, where sunshine will gleam,
With fruits full of humor, a magical dream.
Let's laugh with the leaves, let the fun take its flight,
For joy in the orchard shines ever so bright!

Ripe in Radiance

In a grove where lemons dance,
Oranges wear a cheerful stance.
Limes tell jokes from tree to tree,
While grapefruits laugh, oh so carefree.

A tangerine slipped on a peel,
Yelled, 'Hey, that's not part of the deal!'
The laughter echoed far and wide,
As fruit in sunshine took a ride.

A juicy brawl in the orchard wild,
Grapes got jealous, they were reviled.
They rolled away without a care,
Leaving fruits tangled in the air.

But every squabble turns to cheer,
With fruit punch parties drawing near.
So next time you peel back a zest,
Remember the grove where fun's the best!

The Sunshine Sorbet

There once was a sorbet made of light,
With flavors of sun, oh what a sight!
It giggled as it sat on a cone,
Screaming, 'Lick me, I'm not alone!'

With tarty lemons playing tag,
And sweet oranges waving a flag.
Limes rolled in with a goofy grin,
Shouting, 'Let the fruity games begin!'

Raspberry joined in, a berry so bold,
Claiming the limelight, 'I'm ice cold!'
But all was well in the frosty show,
As they danced together, row by row.

And when the sun began to set,
The sorbet knew it was not done yet.
So it spun on its cone, with flair and joy,
Leaving behind a sweet little ploy!

Burst of Flavor

A fruit bowl filled with vibrant hue,
Jokes were cracked as the melons grew.
Pineapples spiked with humor so bold,
While bananas danced, their peels unrolled.

Limes whispered secrets, quite divine,
While cherries giggled, 'We're on cloud nine!'
Citrus sang in a fruity choir,
Each note a burst, igniting fire.

The grapes rolled in, a wobbly race,
While lemons made faces, quite the ugly grace.
But who would dare halt the fun?
For every slice brought laughter to run!

So gather 'round for a flavor fest,
In fruit we trust, it's simply the best!
With every bite, a giggle to share,
A burst of flavor fills the air!

Citrus Mosaic

In a patchwork grove, colors collide,
Where every fruit wears its pride.
Lemons winked with a zesty glare,
As oranges danced through fragrant air.

Grapefruits spun in a citrus waltz,
Carbonated laughter, never at fault.
While mixed berries joined with a dash of sass,
Painting promises of a flavor blast.

Limes with sunglasses and beachy flair,
Hanging out with tangerines, quite the pair.
They toasted with juice, a tropical treat,
Swirling their shenanigans in the heat.

So if you find yourself near this bliss,
Take a moment, don't let it miss.
In this fruity patch, a mosaic of cheer,
Where every bite brings laughter near!

Nectar of the Sun

When life gives you lemons, just add a twist,
A drink so sweet, it can't be missed.
Squeeze out the giggles, let laughter flow,
Balancing tang with a sunny glow.

In the orchard, oranges do a jive,
Playing hide and seek, oh, how they thrive!
Limes make faces, they're quite the scene,
Like a comedy show, bright and green!

Grapefruits gossip, they love to chat,
Plotting some schemes while wearing a hat.
In a fruit bowl party, they all take flight,
Dancing around, oh, what a sight!

With lemons so zesty, we can't resist,
A prank with a wedge, oh such a twist!
So raise your glass to this fruity fun,
Life's a party under the nectar of the sun!

Lively Fruit Medley

Lemons jest, with their bright sour grin,
Telling jokes with a cheeky spin.
Tangerines whisper, they share a laugh,
Rolling around, they take a bath!

Oranges sing and make a parade,
While grapefruits tumble, shaking their shade.
A pineapple joins, wearing cool shades,
Calling all friends, it's time for charades!

Limes are the pranksters, always in fun,
Throwing zest into every pun.
They squeeze jokes just right, not too tight,
A medley of giggles, it's pure delight!

So gather your fruits, let the laughter flow,
In this juicy party, let's steal the show.
With every slice, we create a new cheer,
A lively concoction of joy is here!

Rind and Rapture

In a world of rinds, humor is ripe,
With oranges chuckling, just take a swipe.
Lemonhead characters, so silly and spry,
Making us giggle whenever they try.

The grapefruits are gossipers, they spill the tea,
Sharing secrets in zestful glee.
But don't let them trick you, they're all in jest,
Playing the fields, and loving the zest.

Tangerines tumble, like small little stars,
Bouncing around, they're our bright avatars.
With a wink and a grin, they jump in delight,
Turning the fruit bowl into pure light!

So crack open the laughter, let flavors ignite,
In a rind of rapture, there's joy to recite.
Every sweet moment is ripe for the pick,
Let's savor the fun with each zesty trick!

The Fragrant Burst

A burst of aroma from citrus delight,
The kitchen's a comedy, oh what a sight!
Limes play the fool, they squirt and they smile,
Creating a chaos that lasts for a while.

Oranges peel back with tales from the grove,
Making us chuckle, sharing their love.
Grapefruits are sly, wearing hats quite absurd,
With every sweet bite, there's laughter unheard.

Lemons join in with their zesty lore,
Slipping on peels, they fall to the floor.
Mixed fruit adventures, all packed in a bowl,
Slicing through giggles, that's how we roll!

So let's toast to the fruits, in a punch so divine,
With laughter and flavor, we joyfully dine.
The fragrant burst fills the air with delight,
This fruity escapade just feels so right!

Tangerine Skies

In the sky, tangy clouds swirl,
Orange laughs, in a playful twirl.
Lemon drops dance with glee,
Sipping sunshine, just you and me.

Limes play hopscotch on the ground,
Giggling like they've just been found.
A zest of cheer in every breeze,
Making us smile with the tease.

Jokes on branches, they twist and bend,
Fruitful laughter, no need to pretend.
Punny puns on every tree,
Nature's joke, come laugh with me.

In the orchard where jokes grow sweet,
Witty fruit, a real treat.
In tangerine skies, we find our way,
Lemonade laughs, come out to play!

Nectar of the Daydreams

Sweet dreams drift on fruity air,
With honeyed zest, we haven't a care.
Imagining juice splashes all around,
Sipping giggles, laughter abound.

In daydreams, fairy fruits take flight,
Floating joy, a curious sight.
Peel back your worries, don't be shy,
Daydreams with nectar, let's fly high.

Comical clouds, with a citrus spree,
Raining down laughter, so carefree.
Sip the sun, in this silly play,
Chasing our giggles, come what may!

So grab a slice of joyful trade,
In realms of dreams, together we wade.
With nectar sweet, let's seize the fun,
Under the glow of a fruity sun!

The Ripple of Citrus Waves

Waves of laughter roll from the shore,
Splashing puns that we can't ignore.
Lemon tides tickle our toes,
Grapefruit smiles in the sunset glow.

Tangerine breezes dance and sway,
Squirting joy in a playful way.
Juicy giggles in the salty spray,
Riding the waves, let's surf all day!

Wobbling fruits float by in glee,
Waves of zesty jubilee.
Who knew that fruit could be this fun?
Riding the ripples, we've just begun!

Here's to the waves that make us sing,
Life's a party, let's dance and swing.
In every splash, we find our cheer,
Bursting with laughter, the coast is clear!

Zing in Every Drop

Oh what fun, a zingy splash,
Dodge the drips, make a dash!
Juicy giggles in every drop,
With every sip, let's make it pop!

Fizzy bubbles of orange cheer,
Lemon laughter, loud and clear.
Pineapple whispers in the fizz,
Making mischief, just like this!

Shake it up, let's twist and shout,
Sour notes in a punchy bout.
Zing through life, with fruity flair,
Lively moments, everywhere!

So raise your glass, let's have a toast,
To zesty drops we love the most.
In every taste, a spark ignites,
With a citrus zing, our spirit lights!

A Orchard's Kiss

In the grove where lemons grow,
I tripped on orange peels below.
A grapefruit danced, I had to stare,
It swirled and twirled, without a care.

The tree declared, 'I'm ripe and round!'
But I just laughed, fell to the ground.
With juice that drips and zest that sings,
Those wobbly fruits wear funny rings.

A tangerine whispered sweet little lies,
'I've got secret plans for the skies!'
I winked back, playing the fool,
Guess I'll bring fruit salad to school!

And when life gives you a lime so bright,
Squeeze it on tacos, oh what a sight!
A burst of laughter, a fruity high,
In this orchard, we'll always fly.

Juicy Reverie

He squeezed an orange, it squirted out,
Hit a passing dog, he wore a pout.
A lime rolled over, a joke on its face,
'You think I'm sour? I'm just in this race!'

Pineapples gossip in their prickly attire,
While mangoes bust out, wishing for fire.
A pomegranate chuckles, its seeds on parade,
Each little burst, a fruity cascade.

Citrus bash, oh what a sight,
Tangerines tango under the light.
Lemons wear hats, with bumbles and jigs,
Life's a circus, thank you, my figs!

So let's blend these fruits in a fizzy delight,
Carbonated dreams take off in flight.
As laughter bubbles, so cheeky and clear,
Let's toast with our glasses, full of good cheer!

The Scent of Citrus Dreams

In a world of zest, we laugh and play,
Dancing with oranges, come join the fray.
Lemons throw confetti, all yellow and cheer,
While limes squeeze giggles, oh dear, oh dear!

A grapefruit wore glasses, sat on a stool,
Reading the news, looking quite cool.
Mandarins giggled, as they spun around,
Their citrusy laughter echoed profound.

A fruit salad party, under the sun,
Everyone's welcome, let's all have fun!
The clock ticks slowly, as flavors collide,
In this fragrant garden, let joy be our guide.

So peel back the laughter, let juices flow,
In this zesty world, smiles always grow.
What a sticky mess on this jubilant team,
Living our lives in a citrusy dream!

Limoncello Lullaby

In a bottle, a lullaby, sweet and light,
A limoncello dream warming the night.
Grapes envy its glow, but truth be told,
Citrus whispers secrets of joy to unfold.

Cuddled up with lemons, all snug and tight,
They giggle and giggle, it's pure delight.
With zesty shenanigans planned for us all,
We're swooning with laughter, we'll dance till we fall!

Slices of fruit on a summer's eve,
Giggles and bubbles, who wouldn't believe?
A strawberry winks, with a sassy salute,
Saying, "I'm berry lucky to share this fruit."

So raise up your glasses, let's laugh and toast,
To the zany fruits we cherish the most!
In this punchy concoction, let joy never shy,
For together we sparkle, oh crunchy and spry!

Sunkissed Elixirs

Bright globes hang from branches high,
A zesty dance under the sky.
Sipping joy from every peel,
Who knew fruit could make you squeal?

Lemonade spills in the sunshine,
Chasing laughter, feeling fine.
A twist of lime, a dash of fun,
Drink it quick before it's done!

Orange slices, stacked like gold,
Tales of sweetness, never old.
With every bite, a giggle flies,
Fruit salad, and we're on the rise!

Lime in hand, a party to fill,
With every sip, a tasty thrill.
Sunkissed joy, a vibrant sight,
Who needs wine when fruit feels right?

A Slice of Joy

A cheeky fruit upon my plate,
Wobbling as I contemplate.
A slice of joy, sharp and sweet,
Each bite's a dance, a fruity treat.

Orange peels like tiny suns,
Twirling laughter, playful runs.
With giggles bursting at the seams,
A fruit bowl filled with silly dreams.

A grapefruit grin, oh what a face,
Juicy zest in every place.
I chuckle as the juices flow,
Squeeze out laughter, watch it grow!

So pass the fruit, let's share the cheer,
With each sweet taste, our joy is clear.
Life is better with a fruity ploy,
A twist of fun, a slice of joy!

The Rind's Retrospective

Once upon a juicy rind,
There lived a zest, so unconfined.
It chuckled loud in sunlit dreams,
Creating laughter, bursting beams.

Memories of tarty traits,
Dancing on the summer plates.
Peel away the dull and dreary,
Fruitful tales, far from weary!

The rind recalls a playful mess,
Squeezed out juice, a laugh caress.
With every splash, a giggle's rise,
Citrusy chuckles light the skies!

So raise your glass to zest gone wild,
Fruits that cheer the inner child.
For every rind holds tales untold,
In sunny sips, we find pure gold.

Flavorful Horizons

On the horizon, flavors bright,
Mocktails shining in the light.
A zesty splash, a fruity fling,
Juicy giggles, let them sing!

Citrusy sunbeams on the rise,
I'm wearing laughter in disguise.
With every sip, a tasty prank,
Fruit bowls filled, let's toast and clank!

Mangoes winking, lemons cheer,
Grapefruit stories bring us near.
Let's tango with a zestful spin,
A flavorful life where jokes begin!

So grab a glass and make a toast,
To fruity fun, let's cheer the most.
With laughter ringing, bold and bright,
Flavorful horizons, pure delight!

www.ingramcontent.com/pod-product-compliance
Lightning Source LLC
Chambersburg PA
CBHW062108280426
43661CB00086B/331